A Day with Firefighters

by Jan Kottke

Children's Press
A Division of Grolier Publishing
New York / London / Hong Kong / Sydney
Danbury, Connecticut

Photo Credits: Cover, p. 5, 7, 9, 11, 19, 21 by Thaddeus Harden; p.13 © Index Stock; p. 15,17 © John Coletti/Index Stock
Contributing Editor: Jennifer Ceaser
Book Design: MaryJane Wojciechowski

Visit Children's Press on the Internet at:
http://publishing.grolier.com

Cataloging-in-Publication Data

Kottke, Jan
    A day with firefighters / by Jan Kottke.
      p.   cm.—(Hard work)
    Includes bibliographical references and index.
     Summary: Simple text and photographs present the work
of firefighters.
    ISBN 0-516-23088-3 (lib. bdg.) — ISBN 0-516-23013-1 (pbk.)
    1. Fire extinction—Juvenile literature   2.   Fire
fighters—Juvenile literature   [1. Fire extinction   2.   Fire
fighters]   I.   Title   II.   Series
      2000
628.9'25—dc21

Contents

We are **firefighters**.

We work at the **fire station**.

4

5

The bell is ringing.

There's a fire somewhere!

Hurry, it is time to go!

I wear a black coat with yellow stripes.

I put on a **helmet.**

9

I open the door to the **fire engine.**

I climb into the front seat.

The fire engine races down the road.

The red lights flash.

The **siren** warns cars to move out of the way.

13

The building is on fire!

There is a lot of smoke.

14

15

I climb the ladder.

I carry a **hose**.

I use the hose to **spray** water on the fire.

17

Now the fire is out.

We worked very hard.

We are tired.

We are also happy.

We like helping people.

We like being firefighters.

21

New Words

fire engine (**en**-jin) a truck that firefighters ride in

firefighters (**fyr**-fi-terz) people who fight fires

fire station (**stay**-shun) a place where firefighters work

helmet (**hel**-met) a hard hat that protects the head

hose (**hoz**) tube that water moves through

siren (**si**-ren) a loud warning sound

spray (**spray**) to put water on something

To Find Out More

Books
All Aboard Fire Trucks
by Freddy Slater
All Aboard Books

Eyewitness Readers: Fire Fighter!
by Angela Royston
DK Publishing

Ms. Murphy Fights Fires
by Alice K. Flanagan
Children's Press

Web Site
Sparky the Fire Dog
http://www.sparky.org
This site has information about firefighters and fire engines.
Help Sparky the Fire Dog practice a fire drill.

Index

About the Author
Jan Kottke is the owner/director of several preschools in the Tidewater area of Virginia. A lifelong early education professional, she is completing a phonics reading series for preschoolers.

Reading Consultants
Kris Flynn, Coordinator, Small School District Literacy, The San Diego County Office of Education

Shelly Forys, Certified Reading Recovery Specialist, W.J. Sahnow Elementary School, Waterloo, IL

Peggy McNamara, Professor, Bank Street College of Education, Reading and Literacy Program